Little Mouse Mat

INSPIRED
PUBLISHING

Author: Kunjuzwa Jezile
Design: Supernatural Creative
Illustrations by Shekinah Flockhart
ISBN 978-1-77630-664-0
First Edition Printing 2021
Published by Inspired Publishing

This book belongs to...

Once upon a time...

not too far away, there was a beautiful field, and in it were creatures who called it their home.

There were big ones and small ones, loud ones and soft ones, scaly ones and furry ones. Living in a cozy nest, right at the edge of the field...

... there was a little mouse called Mat.

Mat lived with his mother, father and sister, Millie.

✗ ✗ ✗

One day, Jackal Jack, who lived
close to Mat heard a noise.

What is that noise?

He stopped fishing and went to see
where it was coming from.

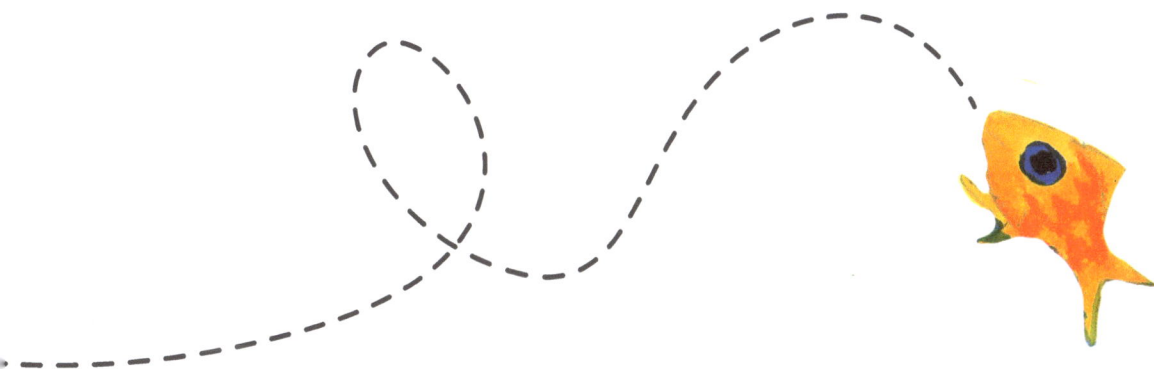

He saw his neighbour, Rabbit Rob who had also heard the
noise and had hopped over to see what was going on.

"Can you hear that noise, Rob?"

"Yes, I can! It's coming from over there!" said Rob.

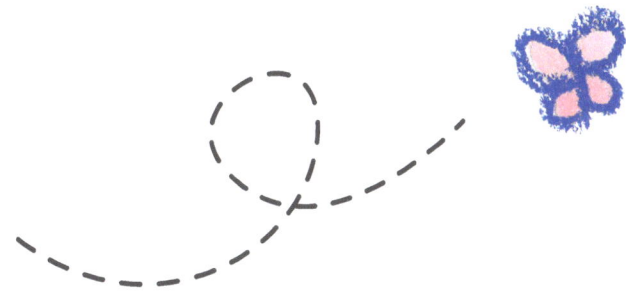

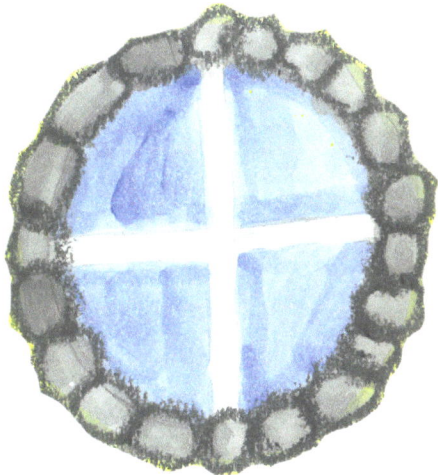

The two neighbours scurried over to where all the noise was coming from.

It was coming from the home of Little Mouse Mat.

Mat was crying!!!!

He was
sobbing and
wailing.

Between the sobs were loud sniffs coming from his
little snout. He was really very upset!

As the neighbours came up next to Mat, Rob put his arm around the little mouse and Jack asked him what was wrong.

"Nobody takes me seriously!" cried Mat. "Nobody wants my help because I am so small. They think that because I'm not big like the other animals, I can't do anything special and that I will put myself in danger."

Rob offered Mat a tissue as he gave another long, loud sniff.

The neighbours looked at each other
and felt the sadness in Mat's heart.
Just then, Rob remembered
something his mom had told him
a long time ago.

"Oh Mat!" exclaimed Rob.
"I remember feeling like you
do. Not so long ago, when I
was a little rabbit."

"No you don't, you are only trying to make me feel better." pouted Mat.

"No, no. My mom told me that every one of us has something special that we are very good at... maybe even the best at. And it's true!

Just as Mat was starting to feel a little better...

...the three friends heard another noise!

Jack just about jumped out of his skin he got such a fright! "What's that noise now?" He said; his eyes wide open with fear. "It's coming from that big tree." said Mat, as he pointed to a giant tree nearby.

They all rushed to the big tree.

It was Dove Daisy making all the noise, and she was beside herself. "What's wrong, Daisy?" asked Rob.

Dove Daisy was so devastated she couldn't speak. With one look at the friends, she fainted".

Pigeon Paul answered, It's our baby, Hope.
She fell into that hole! It's too small, we can't
get in to help her.

Please
help!"

Paul was panicking. " She is still too young.
She can't even walk or see yet.

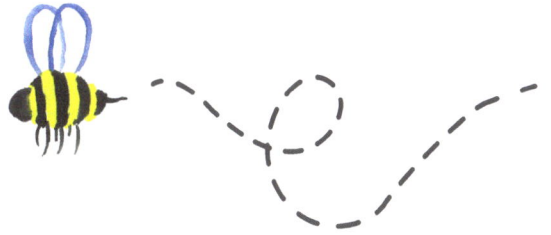

HELP! PLEASE HELP!!!!

By this time, everybody had come to see what
was going on and they were all trying to help.

Giraffe Gab said, "With my long neck I believe I can stretch enough to reach Hope."

Gab tried, but his head was too big to fit inside the hole.

Snake Hissy said, "Let me try,
with my long and thin body,
I believe I can squeeze in."

But the snake's body was too big to fit
into the hole.

Elephant Elle said, "Let me try,
I believe with my long trunk I can
reach inside the hole."

But the hole was too
small for Elle's trunk.

Now they were all panicking!!!

All the animals were trying their best to help but no one could fit inside the hole, it was just too small.

Animals scurried and hopped, flurried and flapped, twisted and stretched. But still little baby Hope was trapped inside the tiny hole.

There was one animal who hadn't tried yet. Mat was seated close by, watching with horror, as every animal tried, and failed, to rescue baby Hope.

Suddenly, Piggy Peggy remembered how they had all teased Mat, and said he was too small to do much.

With a giant SNOOORRRRRTTTT,

Piggy Peggy ran over to Mat and nudged him with her muddy nose.

"Come on Mat!" said Peggy.

"Now is your time to use your special gift. I believe you are the only one who can fit in this little hole!"

"Hurry! Please! We need you!"

All at once, Mat realized his special skill was being small. He was the perfect size to save Hope!

Filled with energy and excitement...

...he leapt up and scampered to the tree as fast as he could.

He ran down that hole so quickly that by the time the other animals knew what was going on, he was already on his way up... with baby Hope!

There were cries of joy all round
and cheers for Mat!

All the animals came around to congratulate him
and thank him for being the hero they had needed
that day. The animals shouted:

"Thank God for little mouse Mat!"

and everybody sang joyfully together. Now that
was a noise to be heard!

While the others sang and danced, Rob quietly came beside Mat and whispered,

"What did I tell you?

We are all special. Big or small, loud or soft, scaly or furry,

every one of us has something special that we are very good at... maybe even the best. A giant grin spread across Mat's mousey face. He was so proud of himself.

Giving his friend a high five, he said, "For the first time, Rob, I don't regret or hate the fact that I'm small. In fact, I'm grateful!"

"We are all special indeed!"

And as the two friends looked out over the celebration, they marveled at how very different everyone is, and how each one was made for something unique, special and amazing.

The End

About the author – Kunjuzwa Jezile

Kunjuzwa Jezile, is a Project Administrator in a Clinical Research Company and has a degree in Financial Information Systems. Kunjuzwa is also a proud wife and mother of two boys.

Regardless of the serious work she does, she is passionate about writing – particularly children's stories that invoke a sense of purpose in the reader.

Through her creative composing of stories and songs, Kunjuzwa aspires to positively impact the lives of both young and old.

www.ingramcontent.com/pod-product-compliance
Lightning Source LLC
Chambersburg PA
CBHW040231070426
42447CB00030B/126